CURAÇAO

ARGO BOOKS

Other ARGO books distributed by De Wit Stores Inc:
Aruba in full Color (with 46 color plates)
St. Maarten in full Color (with 43 color plates)

HANS W. HANNAU

CURAÇAO

IN FULL COLOR

DISTRIBUTORS FOR THE NETHERLANDS ANTILLES:

De Wit Stores Inc., Publishers

ARUBA

ISBN 0-89530-003-6

Printed in Spain

Dep. Legal B-28.384-XIV

INTRODUCTION

Colorful, cosmopolitan, prosperous Curaçao is a happy land, blessed by both nature and the works of man. The clear blue sea that surrounds the island and the silken Caribbean trade winds that caress the land make it a delightful place in which to live, to play and to work. The economy of Curaçao has given it one of the highest standards of living in the western hemisphere. It is Dutch-clean and Dutch-colorful. Luxurious modern resort hotels lure vacationers with all of the most elegant amenities.

Curaçao is the largest of the six islands comprising the Netherlands Antilles. The other five are Aruba, Bonaire, Saba, St. Eustatius and St. Maarten. The capital of the island, Willemstad, is also the seat of government of all the Netherlands Antilles. The island lies off the coast of Venezuela, and is thirty-eight miles long and seven miles wide at its widest. More than half of the 140.000 friendly and candid inhabitants live in Willemstad. These cosmopolitan people represent seventy-nine nationalities.

HISTORY

The first known settlers of Curaçao were the Caiquetios, a tribe of peaceful Arawak Indians. One of the clans of the Caiquetios was called "Curacaos". They were seafarers who conducted a lively traffic with Venezuelan Indians in their slim log canoes.

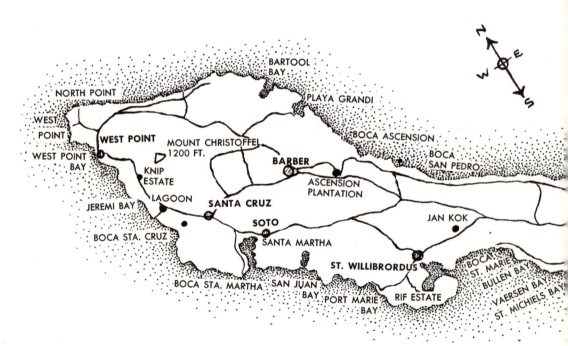

Amerigo Matteo Vespucci, who gave his name to America, was the first white man to set foot on the island, in July, 1499. He was the navigator of a Spanish expedition commanded by Alonso de Ojeda. The Spanish settled Curaçao in 1527, and there raised cattle for the export of hides. They remained until they were harried by the Dutch into abandoning the island to the Netherlands in 1634.

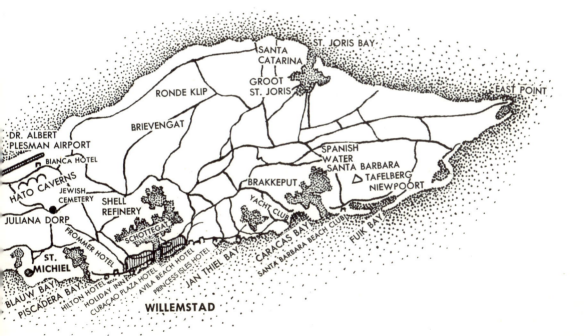

To Curaçao in 1642 came Peter Stuyvesant, who had been appointed Director of Curaçao, and it was here that he left a leg, which was amputated because of a wound received in the blockade of St. Maarten island. Tradition has it that Stuyvesant's leg is buried in the cemetery at Monte Verde on Curaçao. From Curaçao he left to become Director-General in New Amsterdam, now New York.

Among the very first settlers were the Jews, who were fleeing the Spanish and Portuguese Inquisition. These refugees found shelter among the tolerant Dutch in Curaçao, just as the philosopher Spinoza's family found shelter in Holland. The Jews contributed greatly to the economic and cultural enrichment of the community, and at one time were the majority of the white population. The community of Mikve Israel was established in 1651, and the community's cemetery of Beth Haim, used since 1659, is the oldest Jewish cemetery in the western world.

During the seventeenth century Louis XIV of France made several unsuccessful attempts to conquer Curaçao, and these forays kept the colony militarily in readiness. Two slave uprisings, in 1750 and in 1795, broke the relative peace of the eighteenth century. Slavery was ultimately abolished in 1863. In 1807, during the Napoleonic Wars, Curaçao was occupied by the British, but it was returned to the Netherlands in 1816 and has remained a part of the Kingdom of the Netherlands ever since.

Curaçao maintained a sleepy existence until the discovery of oil in Venezuela in 1914. In the following year, the Royal Dutch Shell Company (correctly, the N. V. Curaçaosche Petroleum Industrie Maatschappij, an associated company) began to build one of the world's largest oil refineries on the island. The attractions were its stable government and a fine port. The refinery brought economic vitality to the island, and it has since then become a hub of commerce and shipping. Fleets of tankers bring crude oil daily from Lake Maracaibo to be refined and then reshipped in ocean-going tankers to all parts of the world.

Peter Stuyvesant Statue
Curaçao

Prosperity brought a great influx of workers from half a hundred nations. North American, Dutch, British, Spanish, Portuguese, Venezuelans, Hindus, West and East Indians, Chinese and many other nationalities have created a polyglot microcosm. Many tongues are spoken, and Dutch is the official language. But the real language of Curaçao is Papiamento, the lingua franca of the Leeward Islands. Papiamento has roots in Dutch, Spanish, French, Portuguese, English and African. The United States has contributed "payday", "okay" and "watch out". Papiamento was in existence in the early eighteenth century. Its grammar is simple, but to this day it has no fixed spelling.

Shell Refinery
Curaçao

Autonomy Monument and Amstel Brewery

SIGHTSEEING

The weather is almost always perfect in Curaçao. There is little rainfall —a scant twenty-two inches a year. The skies are almost always sunny, and the cool breeze of the trade winds blows almost constantly. In other words, it is an idyllic country for sightseeing.

The sightseeing tour begins in the colorful capital city, Willemstad. The first point of interest is the Queen Emma Bridge (Koningin Emma Brug), which spans St. Anna Bay and links the two parts of the city, Punda and Otrobanda. Otrobanda means "the other side". The bridge floats on sixteen great pontoons, and sways enough to make some people seasick when they walk across it. It is swung aside some twenty times a day to let ships pass in and out of the harbor, causing pedestrians to scramble and motorists to sit stuck in traffic jams. The bridge used to be a toll bridge, the user being charged according to his ability to pay —five cents if he was wealthy enough to own shoes, two cents if he wore sandals, and nothing if he was barefoot. Human nature is such that the very poor tried to get sandals, and the middling poor to get shoes. All wanted to pay, to show that they were better off than they actually were.

One way of not having to wait for the Queen Emma to close is to take the little Dutch ferryboat, veerboot (not to be confused with the German word verboten, which means "forbidden"). The ferry shuttles back and forth across the bay like a water bug while the bridge is open.

The attractive gabled houses on the Punda side of the city suggest seventeenth century Amsterdam or Rotterdam, but the colors are Caribbean. They are painted in all the pastel shades: lilac, purple, violet, indigo, plum, apricot, aquamarine, emerald, magenta, chocolate, terra cotta. There is only one old house that is white, and thereon hangs a tale. The story goes that it was forbidden by ordinance to paint houses white after one governor was troubled by headaches which he attributed to the glare of white houses. He decreed that only soft colors were to be used henceforth.

The fairy-tale charm of Willemstad is enhanced by the colorful "Floating Markct" of schooners on the little canal leading to the Waaigat, a small yacht basin. Fruits, vegetables and fabrics are displayed on docked boats that have come from Venezuela, Colombia and other Caribbean lands.

(continued on page 33)

St. Anna Bay with Fort Amsterdam and the Hotel Curaçao Plaza

La Bahía de Sta. Anna con el Fuerte Amsterdam y el Hotel Curaçao Plaza

13

Inside Fort Amsterdam
Dentro del Fuerte Amsterdam

Red Hibiscus
Hibisco Rojo

The New Queen Juliana Bridge over St. Anna Bay

El Nuevo Puente Queen Juliana sobre la Bahía de Sta. Anna

Natives of Curaçao
in their Colorful
Costumes

Nativos de Curaçao
en sus ropas
de mucho colorido

→
De Ruyter Plein (Punda)

16

Corner of Handelskade and Breedestraat
La esquina de Handelskade y Breedestraat

→

Business Section of Punda (Willemstad)
Barrio Comercial de Punda (Willemstad)

Pool Terrace, Holiday Inn
La terraza de la piscina del Holiday Inn

← *Curaçao Hilton Hotel*

21

*View over Waaigat to
Post Office and Punda*

*Vista por arriba del Waaigat
hacia el Correo y la Punda*

Floating Market, Punda

El Mercado Flotante →

Landhuis Ascension

←

Countryside with St. Christoffel Mountain (1230 feet)

El campo con la Montaña St. Christoffel (1230 piés)

Wine Cellar, Landhuis Jan Kock

Bodega vinícola, Landhuis Jan Kock

*Westpoint, Beach
and Town*

*Westpoint, la Playa
y el Pueblo*

*Santa Martha Bay with
Its Beautiful Beaches*

→

*La Bahía de Santa Marta
con sus bellas playas*

←

*Santa Barbara Beach
at Spanish Water*

*La Playa Santa Barbara
en Spanish Water*

Description of foregoing color photographs

Cover Picture

Air View of Willemstad, Capital of Curaçao

Uniquely Dutch and definitely European is the city of Willemstad. The picture shows some of the ancient fortifications, with the Waterfort to the right. This fortress has been converted into a modern resort hotel of imposing dimensions, the Curaçao Plaza. The city faces the Caribbean Sea. To the left is St. Anna Bay, with the Queen Emma Pontoon Bridge leading from the city section of Punda to Otrobanda on the other side of the bay.

Page 13

St. Anna Bay with Fort Amsterdam and the Hotel Curaçao Plaza

A tanker passes through St. Anna Bay with a load of oil from the Shell refinery. The square behind is ancient Fort Amsterdam, lodging many government offices and facing the waterfront with the Governor's residence (gray roof). Behind to the right is the Hotel Curaçao Plaza. with its big new tower, built into the old Waterfort.

Page 14.

Inside Fort Amsterdam

The picture shows the courtyard of Fort Amsterdam, built by the Dutch shortly after they took the island from the Spaniards (1635-1675), In the back is the old Fort-church (Dutch Reformed Church), now the United Protestant Church, rebuilt in 1763.

Red Hibiscus

Growing all over Curaçao is the Red Hibiscus (Hibiscus rosa-sinensis), a native of China. The attractive red flowers, blooming only for one day, reach a size of five inches in diameter.

Page 15.

The New Queen Juliana Bridge

Like a tremendous arch the new Queen Juliana Bridge overlooks the capital city, leading over St. Anna Bay and connecting Otrobanda with Punda. In front of the photograph is Punda with Fort Amsterdam, now modernized to Government offices, behind St. Anna Bay and in the background part of the Shell Refinery.

Page 16.

Natives of Curaçao in Their Colorful Costumes

The people of Curaçao cultivate the traditions of their island, wearing old costumes, and preserving traditional music and dances.
The couple in the picture are members of a folklore group of singers and dancers who perform from time to time in the city.

Page 17.

De Ruyter Plein (Punda)

Looking over the Waaigat from Scharloo to Punda, this romantic little square of Willemstad, surrounded by typical Dutch buildings, is visible.

Page 18.

Corner of Handelskade and Breedestraat

A beautiful and typical Dutch scene in the business section of Punda is the corner of Handelskade and Breedestraat, shown in this picture. The building in the center is the Penha Building, which dates back to the eighteenth century. To the left is Handelskade along St. Anna Bay, and leading into the background is Breedestraat, main artery of the business section, with leading stores such as Spritzer & Fuhrmann, Penha, Wooden Shoe, Kan Jewellers, Van Dorp, El Globo and others.

Page 19.

Business Section of Punda (Willemstad)

This photograph is a dramatic air view into the narrow streets of the old business section of Willemstad, with its red-roofed, picturesque old Dutch buildings, St. Anna Bay to the left, and Waaigat in the background.

Page 20.

The Curaçao Hilton Hotel

One of the best new resort hotels of Curaçao is the Hilton, with a beautiful beach and swimming pool, night club, casino, shopping arcade and two hundred guest rooms. The air view shows clearly the attractive layout of the hotel, located on the leeward (southwest) coast of the island just a few miles west of Willemstad.

Page 21.

Pool Terrace, Holiday Inn

The two hundred room Holiday Inn of Curaçao is a top resort hotel. Located on the leeward coast close to Willemstad, it has a beautiful pool terrace, attractive gardens, a casino, night club and shopping alley.

Page 22.

View over Waaigat to Post Office and Punda

Looking from the hills of Scharloo over the Waaigat to Punda, one sees in the center of the photograph the modern post office, just behind a church-like building, the Reformed Temple Emanuel, and, stretching to the horizon, the Caribbean Sea.

Page 23 (also lower picture Page 22)

Floating Market, Punda

Along De Ruyterkade on Waaigat is the picturesque Floating Market, where visiting merchant schooners from the South American mainland and from neighboring islands offer vegetables, fruit and handicrafts directly from their ships. The sails are used as awnings to cover the goods and to protect them against sun and rain.

Page 24.

Countryside with St. Christoffel Mountain (1230 feet)

This air view shows the northwestern part of Curaçao around St. Cruz where the countryside (cunucu) is green and fertile. In the background is St. Christoffel Mountain. Agricultural revenues of the island are very small, except for certain local oranges which are used to make the famous Curaçao liqueur. Also, aloe plantations (Aloe vera) still bring good returns.

Page 25.

Landhuis Ascension

There are many old plantation houses, dating back to the eighteenth century, such as Ascension. They are most numerous in the western part of Curaçao. They were agricultural centers but were also involved in salt production and the slave trade. Many of them, like Ascension, were strongly fortified against marauding pirates and slave insurrections of the time.

Wine Cellar, Landhuis Jan Kock

Not far to the west of Willemstad is the landhuis Jan Kock at Willibrordus. The old country house was built in the seventeenth century, principally for salt production in the nearby salt ponds. The salt was transported by sail to Holland for the herring fishery. The heavy furniture of the wine cellar is made out of trunks of mahogany trees that grew on the old plantation. Torches, ancient lanterns and local music create a fantastic atmosphere for serving wine with bread and cheese in the evening. In the daytime it is a pleasure to look around from the wellrestored terrace of the country house to get an idea of how a salt plantation was run more than 200 years ago.

Page 26.

Santa Bárbara Beach at Spanish Water

One of the finest public beaches of Curaçao is Santa Barbara Beach at Spanish Water, just a few miles east of Willemstad.

Page 27.

Westpoint, Beach and Town

Far to the west of the island is the village of Westpoint, which has a nice beach on the leeward coast.

Santa Martha Bay with Its Beautiful Beaches

A fine beach development is located at Santa Martha Bay on the leeward coast in the western part of the island. There is the attractive Coral Cliff Hotel with thirty-five modern guest rooms. A hundred-room hotel is also planned there, under the management of the Executive House Hotels.

Page 28.

Table Mountain

Just east of Willemstad is the picturesque Table Mountain, background for many boat and sailboat races from Spanish Water.

(continued from page 12)

Almost every point of interest in the city is within walking distance of the center. Of great interest is the old Dutch Reformed Church, rebuilt in 1763 within Fort Amsterdam. Embedded in its walls is a cannonball fired by the English in 1804. The best view of the city is obtained from the Franklin D. Roosevelt house, built by the people of the island in gratitude for protection during World War II. It was presented to the U.S. Government and is now the official residence of the U.S. Consul General.

The Mikve Israel Synagogue, oldest in the Western Hemisphere, dates back to 1732. This exciting example of eighteenth century Dutch architecture is quite close to the floating market. Fresh sand is sprinkled over the floor of the temple daily as a symbol of the wandering of the Israelites in the Egyptian desert during the Exodus. Immense brass chandeliers are replicas of those in the famous Portuguese Synagogue in Amsterdam.

West of the city is the Beth Haim (House of the Living) Jewish cemetery, consecrated in 1659, and the oldest Caucasian burial place still in use in the New World. More than 1700 tombstone carvings from the seventeenth and eighteenth century, still legible, present a fascinating record of those early refugees from persecution.

In Otrobanda is the Curaçao Museum, with a large collection of interesting pieces of Indian (Caiquetios) culture in the basement. Antiques, paintings of the colonial era, and objets d'art of an earlier day are also on display in the museum.

Four interesting statues in Willemstad evoke the history of Curaçao. Peter Stuyvesant, in the garden of Stuyvesant college, looks determined enough to conquer the whole of the New World for Holland. The second statue is that of Simón Bolívar, the South American liberator, who did so much to cement relations between Curaçao and Venezuela. These happy relations are a factor of particular importance in view of Venezuela's oil, Curaçao's refineries, and the migration of Venezuelans to Curaçao. The third statue is that of Pedro Luis Brión, which dominates Brionplein (Brión Square) at the Otrobanda end of the Queen Emma Bridge. Born in Curaçao in 1782, he was instrumental, as Admiral of the Colombian fleet under Bolívar, in winning freedom for Colombia and Venezuela. Although a Curaçaon he was buried in the National Pantheon in Caracas at the request of the Venezuelan Government.

The fourth statue is of Manuel Carlos Piar. Born in Otrobanda in 1777, he was the first non-Venezuelan to become a Venezuelan general. He was the conqueror of Guiana and victor in some famous battles. His statue stands on Plaza Piar in Punda.

The Fortified Brievengat Landhuis

St. Christoffel Mountain

THE COUNTRYSIDE

Outside Willemstad, the countryside has a charm all its own. Here cactus plants grow twenty feet high, and the crowns of the weird divi-divi trees all stream downwind. These distinctive trees grow to a height of ten feet, and then thrust out trunk and branches at a right angle from the trunk for another ten feet or more; they appear to be growing sideways, paralleling the wind, rather than vertically.

Generally the countryside is dry. In picturesque thatched huts and adobe homes families weave straw and pound meal, and on the coast the native fishermen cast their nets. Occasionally, a handsome colonial estate, or landhuis, emerges, inviting investigation.

Guided tours lead all the way to the northwestern tip of the island and along the north coast. En route there is Boca Tabla, a grotto carved out by the pounding sea on the windward coast. There are excellent beaches on the sheltered leeward (southwestern) coast at Knip Bay, Piscadera Bay, Spanish Water, Santa Marta, Santa Cruz, and Westpoint; the last-named is a twenty-five mile drive from Willemstad. Here, too, are the remains of an old stone settlement, a fishing village, and the bluest water imaginable. Tours are also arranged to the Hato Caves, where modern man has gone in for cave painting. In this subterranean locality, colored lights play on scenes from the Arabian Nights, Snow White and the Seven Dwarfs, Sinbad the Sailor, a Persian Market, and other fanciful subjects. Here also are great stalactites and stalagmites.

Ancient Straw covered Home at San Pedro

The Curaçao Hilton

HOTELS IN CURAÇAO

Before the erection of the Hotel Curaçao Plaza (formerly Inter Continental), accommodations in Willemstad were so limited that few tourists stayed on the islands for more than a day or so. The advent of this luxurious hotel in the Intercontinental chain in 1957 lured more visitors to stay longer. Built right into the old seaside fort that was constructed by the Dutch in 1827 — the massive walls are thirty-three feet thick — the Curaçao Plaza is a happy blend of site and architecture. The ramparts of the fort now serve as a promenade for guests. They form an arc, partly facing the open sea, with surf pounding at the base of the fort, and partly facing the narrow channel leading to the harbor. Boats pass so close that guests can easily exchange remarks with the officers and crew.

The hotel has 244 air-conditioned double rooms and a splitlevel swimming pool with portholes on the lower level through which non-swimmers can see the bathers. There is a coffee shop, excellent restaurants, chic bars, a nightclub, and a lively gambling casino — a touch of Las Vegas in the tropics.

The success of the Intercontinental inspired the building of additional hostelries. The Curaçao Hilton opened in 1967, with two hundred ultra-modern guest rooms. It is situated on a beautiful beach on Piscadera Bay. There is also a luxurious gambling casino, glass-enclosed outside elevators, excellent convention facilities, restaurants, bars, shops, a swimming pool, and all the comforts for which Hilton is famous.

Close by is the newest hotel in Curaçao, the Arthur Frommer Hotel, with one hundred rooms, ninety villas and all modern conveniences.

The Holiday Inn has been popular ever since it opened in 1968. It is located close to town, directly on the ocean, and has two hundred rooms, an olympic size swimming pool, beautiful gardens, an elegant dining room and an attractive casino.

The Princess Isles Hotel, built in 1967 on the south coast near Willemstad, has a fine beach, 138 rooms, a huge swimming pool and cabana club, a casino and most modern facilities.

The Country Inn, a motel with seventy-two cozy, air-conditioned rooms with kitchenette, refrigerator, television and radio, is near Willemstad. There is a swimming pool, cafeteria, self-service barbecue, tennis, volleyball, midget golf, bolas criollas, and a children's playground on the premises.

The Coral Cliff Hotel, on a secluded beach on Santa Martha Bay twenty-four miles northwest of Willemstad, has thirty-five air-conditioned rooms, all with balconies overlooking the bay. There is a marina, an observatory, deep-sea fishing, water skiing, snorkeling, sailing, tennis, and much more.

There is a nice commercial hotel in Willemstad, the San Marco, with seventy-five rooms. A small but attractive motel-type hostelry near the airport is "La Bianca", with twenty rooms.

Hotel Arthur Frommer, newest in Curaçao

CURAÇAO CUISINE

Eating can be an adventure in Curaçao. In addition to the very fine restaurants in the hotels, there is the attractive Fort Nassau Restaurant, built into a hilltop fortress overlooking the Schottegat.

The basic Curaçao cuisine is Dutch and may have Indonesian and Chinese complements. A justly famous dish is honden portie —hound's portion— which consists of a hero-sized filet mignon, a hill of rice topped by two fried eggs, French fries, tomatoes, peppers, fish flakes, asparagus, and several Javanese spices.

Another is the famous rijsttafel, or rice table, which has a basic mountain of rice and twenty to forty assorted side dishes. Exceedingly delicious is a kind of Dutch pea soup called erwtensoep, as thick as the oil refined in Curaçao, which may be followed by a gevulde kaas (a filled cheese of the Edam variety). The nearest thing to a national dish is funchi, the Caribbean tortilla, which is served with meat and is used to soak up the rich Dutch gravies.

Since Curaçao is so cosmopolitan, the gourmet can also enjoy French, Italian, German, Austrian, Chinese, North American and even Irish cuisines — to name but a few.

Famous throughout the world is the liqueur, Curaçao, that is named for the island. This is, of course, the specialty of the island and is made from the peel of indigenous oranges. No other Caribbean island has been able to produce the liqueur, for only Curaçao seems able to produce the special kind of orange needed.

(continued on page 61)

Town Hall, Willemstad   El Ayuntamiento de Willemstad

41

Along Breedestraat (Punda)

→

*Bolivar House,
View from
Avila Hotel Beach*

*La Casa Bolívar,
vista de la Playa
del Hotel Avila*

A lo largo de la calle Breedestraat (Punda)

42

Mikve Israel, Oldest Jewish Synagogue in the Western World (1732)

Mikve Israel, la sinagoga judía más vieja del mundo occidental (1732)

WILLEMSTAD

Beth Haim, Oldest Jewish Cemetery in the Western World (1659)

Beth Haim, el cementerio judío más viejo del Mundo Occidental (1659)

Interior, Oldest Jewish Synagogue in the Western World

Interior de la sinagoga judía más vieja del mundo occidental

Ancient Jewish Gravestones, Curaçao

Viejísimas lápidas sepulcrales judías

*New "Queen Elizabeth II"
Moored in Caracas
Bay*

*La nueva nave "Queen
Elizabeth II" anclada en
la Bahía de Caracas*

In the Harbor

En la bahía

→

*Fort Beekenburg
at the Entrance
of Caracas Bay*

*El Fuerte
Beekenburg, a la
entrada de la
Bahía de Caracas*

View from Fort Nassau
*Vista desde
el Fuerte Nassau*

*The Romance of an
Oil Refinery*

*El romance de una
refinería de petróleo*

When Night Comes...
Al anochecer...

Old Home on Scharloo Weg (1791)
Casa antigua en Scharloo Weg (1791)

Frangipani, a Flowering Tree of Curaçao

Franchipán, un árbol florído de Curaçao

Street Café, Willemstad

Cafés callejeros en Willemstad

Wilhelmina Park, Punda

Curaçao Museum

El Parque Wilhelmina, Punda

El Museo de Curaçao

In the Country Inn
En el Country Inn

→

On Santa Barbara Beach

En la Playa Santa Bárbara

Princess Isles Hotel

52

Curaçaoans Like Music and Dancing

A los nativos de Curaçao les gusta la música y el baile

54

Description of foregoing pictures

Page 41.

Town Hall, Willemstad

Just behind Fort Amsterdam on Wilhelmina Park the Town Hall is located. It is the seat of the Courts of Justice, and here on the second Tuesday of May the 22 representatives of all Netherlands Antilles meet every year.

Page 42.

Along Breedestraat (Punda)

This main shopping street in Willemstad has a colorful line of old Dutch houses interspersed with modern structures. The modern buildings are designed to harmonize with the old.

Page 43.

Bolivar House, View from Avila Hotel Beach

Simón Bolivar's sisters lived in the tower-like octagonal house, and here Bolivar himself joined them when he visited Curaçao in 1812. The foreground shows the beach of the Avila Beach Hotel, a romantic hotel that was formerly a Governor's palace and now has modern conveniences,

air-conditioned rooms, restaurant, schooner bar, and a beautiful garden directly on a private beach.

Pages 44-45.

Mikve Israel, Oldest Jewish Synagogue in the Western World (1732)

Willemstad has one of the oldest Jewish settlements in the Americas. Its first inhabitants were refugees from the Spanish and Portuguese Inquisitions who came to Curaçao in the middle of the seventeenth century. The first synagogue was built in 1685, enlarged and rebuilt in 1692 and 1703. The present Mikve Israel Synagogue was built in 1730-32, and looks today just like it did then.

Beth Haim, Oldest Jewish Cemetery in the Western World (1659)

There are 2.568 ancient grave stones here, many with interesting inscriptions, mostly in Portuguese. In this oldest Jewish cemetery, on the outskirts of Willemstad, rests Elias H. Touro, who died in 1674. The famous Touro Synagogue in Newport, Rhode Island, was named after his grandnephew, Judah Touro.

Page 46.

In the Harbor

The interesting air view shows part of the extensive harbor of Curaçao.

Page 47.

"Queen Elizabeth II" Moored in Caracas Bay

The photograph shows this luxurious cruise ship in Caracas Bay, Curaçao. To the right on the cliff is the customs office.

Fort Beekenburg at the Entrance of Caracas Bay

One of Curaçao's ancient forts of the eighteenth century, Fort Beekenburg is still in good condition. An attack on this fort by the British in 1805 was beaten off.

Page 48.

The Romance of an Oil Refinery

With all of its modern and technical structures, the large Shell Oil Refinery offers a romance of its own, especially in the evening, when thousands of lights and flames shine and glow against the dark sky. It is a great experience to look down on the refinery from Fort Nassau (built in 1796), now an excellent restaurant, at night time. It looks more like a big city, with all its lights and a certain halo above it.

Page 49.

Old Home on Scharloo Weg (1791)

Many of the most attractive old homes are in Scharloo. This eighteenth century residence is typical of many more in this section of Willemstad.

Page 50.

Frangipani, a Flowering Tree of Curaçao

Fragrance and beauty have made this small tree a favorite for planting in the gardens of Curaçao, where it thrives. The Latin name is Plumeria rubra, after the French botanist Charles Plumier. This tree is a native of the West Indies and tropical America, but is also found in Ceylon, India, and in Hawaii, where it is especially popular because its blossoms are used for leis to adorn visitors' necks.

Street Café, Willemstad

Willemstad looks like a little Amsterdam, with its Dutch houses and gables, street cafés, waterways and narrow streets. The pictured street café is in the heart of the Punda shopping district.

Page 51.

Wilhelmina Park, Punda

In the center of the old city between Breede Straat and the old city walls, is Wilhelmina Park with a fine statue of Queen Wilhelmina in white marble. Just behind the statue is the Jewish Reform Temple Emanuel, looking more like a church than a synagogue. The city walls are visible to the right of the temple.

Curaçao Museum

This fine collection of West Indian relics of Curaçao includes also old Dutch furniture, musical instruments, slave bells. It is housed in an old Dutch quarantine station in Otrobanda, which was built in 1853.

Page 52

In the Country Inn

Country Inn is in every respect a good and pleasant motel, not only for the travelling businessman, but also for longer stays, especially for family vacations. Its attractions include kitchenettes, refrigerators, children's playground, midget golf, bolas criollas, tennis and a fine swimming pool and terrace on its own premises, with seventy-two air conditioned rooms.

Princess Isles Hotel

Just outside of town to the east of Willemstad, this hotel has a fine beach on the leeward coast. It is a modern, attractive resort built in 1967, with 138 air-conditioned rooms. There is a large swimming pool, a cabana club, casino, bars and dining room.

Page 53.

On Santa Barbara Beach

The favorite public beach is the splendid stretch of sand at St. Barbara, not far to the east of Willemstad.

Page 54.

Curaçaoans Like Music and Dancing

The people of Curaçao have always liked music. There is a school of music and the dance bands are popular. When the bands play for old folk dances, they quite often use old instruments, such as those in the upper picture. They wear traditional costumes when they dance some of their old native dances, and these can be seen in the lower picture.

Page 55.

Spanish Water

Looking over Spanish Water, a lagoon east of Willemstad, offers a view of its beaches, islands, peninsulas, weekend colonies. It is headquarters for water sports, boating, sailing, fishing and the Curaçao Yacht Club. The Table Mountain dominates the background. There is an outlet to the ocean through Spanish Bay, which adjoins Caracas Bay and provides superb anchorage for large and small boats.

Page 56.

Evening at the Schottegat

Sunsets and evenings can be beautifully colorful in Curaçao. This view from the old Pareira Pier to Fort Nassau, silhouetted to the left, shows in the background the outline of the hills of the Three Brothers and a tanker to the right.

(continued from page 40)

SHOPPING

Low import duties have made Curaçao a bargain center for luxury merchandise in the Caribbean. It is virtually a free port. Most of the shops are in Punda, the oldest part of Willemstad. The beautiful merchandise displayed, such as Swiss watches, French perfumes, china, porcelains, silver, crystal, cameras, binoculars, Oriental silks, diamonds, and so much more is difficult to resist. Many Curaçao shopkeepers keep open on Sundays and holidays when cruise ships are in port.

Breedestraat, a Fine Shopping Street

61

SPORTS

Curaçao is well known to sports lovers. It offers a great variety, and its waters are among the finest in the world for undersea exploration. Active sports include sailing, fishing, diving, scuba diving, snorkeling, swimming, water skiing, tennis and bowling. Golfers may use the Shell Golf Course upon payment of a greens fee, and there is also horseback riding.

Spectator sports are soccer, baseball, and occasional tennis matches featuring internationally known tennis pros.

Native Musician

OUTLOOK FOR CURAÇAO

As part of the Netherlands Antilles, Curaçao is an active partner with Holland and her sister islands in the Caribbean for mutual economic development. The political framework of the Netherlands Antilles is that of a parliamentary democracy, the individual islands exercising independent power in many fields. Universal suffrage is enjoyed by men and women. Curaçao enjoys political stability and peace.

The principal source of Curaçao's prosperity today is the extensive oil-refining operation. International trade and international transport are playing an ever-increasing role in the island's international economy. Of great significance, too, is the rapidly growing tourist business, emanating not only from North and South America but also from Europe.

To maintain and develop further this high level of prosperity, Curaçao has undertaken a ten-year plan of development, now in the second half stage, for the purpose of improving labor relations and conditions, increasing the supply of energy, fuel, and water, developing ever-better transportation and communications within the island, and promoting tourism, all with the ultimate happiness of its citizenry in mind. No island in the Caribbean has a brighter future than Curaçao.

ACKNOWLEDGMENTS

In preparing this book I had the valuable cooperation of the Curaçao Government Tourist Bureau and of Fred Fischer of Curaçao, a photographer of great talent and ability.

Hans W. Hannau